Investing Made Easy

A Step-by-Step Handbook for Beginners

by

Adam S. Williams

Table of contents

Introduction

A strong grasp of investing is the first step towards accumulating money and achieving financial independence in the fast-paced world of finance. With the beginner investor in mind, this extensive guide provides a simple and easy-to-follow road map for navigating the intricacies of the investing world.

This book aims to simplify the process and provide you with the necessary information to make well-informed choices, regardless of whether you're new to the world of finance or want to improve your investing approach. "Investing Made Easy" is your go-to resource for realizing the full potential of your money, from setting the groundwork with fundamental investing principles to assisting you via doable, step-by-step methods.

Learn how to make reasonable financial objectives, and get knowledge about different investing options. By using approachable language and real-world examples, we want to turn what may first appear like a difficult task into a fun and fulfilling journey. Whether your objective is to prepare for a long-term retirement plan, a dream trip, or a down payment on a house, this manual gives you the skills you need to effectively navigate the financial markets. Come along on this educational trip with us as we help you lay the groundwork for a bright financial future by simplifying difficult investing ideas into easily understood insights. More than simply a manual, "Investing Made Easy" is your partner in the world of investing, arming you with the information and self-assurance you need to take charge of your financial future. Together, let's take this powerful journey and simplify investing for you.

Chapter 1

The Fundamentals of Investing

Investing is the act of purchasing assets that appreciate over time and provide capital gains or income payments.
In a wider sense, investment may also be about spending time or money to enhance your own life or the lives of others. However, buying stocks, real estate, and other valuable goods to make financial gains or generate income is known as investing in the world of finance.

Investing, in general, is the process of using money to labor for a while on a project or endeavor to make positive returns (i.e., earnings that surpass the amount of the original investment).

Investing may take various forms (directly or indirectly). For example, one might use capital to launch a company or buy assets like real estate to rent it out and/or sell it at a profit in the future.

Investing is not the same as saving since the money employed is put to work, which implies that there is an inherent risk that the associated project or projects might fail and result in a financial loss. Speculation is different from investing in that the latter involves wagering on short-term price swings rather than putting the money to work.

The act of investing is the distribution of resources, usually monetary, with the hope of making a profit or income in the future. Investing is a deliberate commitment with the long-term goal of building wealth, not just spending money. A variety of financial products, such as stocks, bonds, property, mutual funds, and others, may be invested in.

Investing is primarily done to increase wealth by allocating funds to assets that have the potential to increase in value or provide income. In addition to maintaining the value of money, the objective is to actively and increase it by deliberate and well-informed decision-making.

Recognizing Investment's Part in Financial Growth

Building long-term wealth and attaining financial development is mostly dependent on investing.

Here are the main facets of its function:

- Wealth Accumulation: Investing provides the chance for capital growth, which enables people to gradually acquire wealth. Investors may take advantage of the power of compounding and see an exponential increase in the value of their original investment by carefully selecting assets with growth potential.

- Income Generation: Regular income in the form of dividends or interest is provided by certain assets, such as stocks or bonds that pay dividends. This revenue stream adds to a varied and long-lasting financial portfolio whether reinvested or used to cover short-term expenses.

- Hedging Against Inflation: Inflation erodes the buying power of money over time. Investments serve as a buffer against this loss, particularly those that outperform rates of inflation. Investments that are resistant to inflation include tangible assets like real estate or stakes in businesses with significant growth potential.

- Reaching Financial Objectives: Investing may help you reach short- or long-term financial objectives. By increasing their wealth throughout the chosen time horizon, an investing plan that has been properly designed may assist people in reaching their goals, whether they are saving for a house, school, or retirement.

- Retirement Planning: A key element of retirement planning is investing. Throughout a person's career, diversifying one's portfolio might provide income in retirement, assuring one's financial stability in later years.

- Creating Financial Independence: People may become financially independent via successful investment. By creating passive income streams and building wealth, people may become less reliant on regular jobs and have more freedom to follow their hobbies and passions.

- Risk management: Although there is always some risk associated with investing, hazards may be reduced and managed with the support of a well-diversified portfolio. Investing across a variety of asset classes helps investors reduce the effect of a single investment's bad performance.

The distinctions between Investing and Saving

To guarantee financial stability and a promising future, it is important to comprehend the difference between saving and investing. Even though these phrases are sometimes used synonymously, it's crucial to understand that they are not the same. Starting early is a fantastic approach to position oneself for long-term financial security. Savings and investing are both essential components of personal finance. To assist you in better comprehending these ideas, we will go over what investing and saving.

How Does One Save?

Individuals save aside money for emergencies as well as for shopping. Setting money away for future needs is called saving, and it is a crucial component of personal finance. Consider it like investing in a piggy bank, only you may use a savings account or a certificate of deposit (CD) that accrues interest over time instead of a real piggy bank. One may save money for several purposes, such as purchasing a new device, planning a trip, or setting aside money for unforeseen costs in an emergency fund.

Saving money is a great method to reach short-term financial objectives and be ready for unforeseen events like auto repairs or medical expenses. Regular savings can help you build a cushion that will support you during difficult times. Although the return rates on savings are often modest, your money is still secure since they are low-risk investments.

An illustration

Putting some of your allowance or salary into a savings account each month is one way to save. For example, let's imagine you have ten months to save up to $2,000 for a new laptop. You may achieve your goal without having to pay interest on a credit card or loan by saving away $200 a month.

To guarantee that you continuously save without needing to remember to do it manually, you may also utilize automated transfers.

Benefits and Drawbacks of Saving

Savings provide many advantages, including being protected from loss, having cash on hand for purchases and other short-term objectives, and acting as a safety net against unforeseen expenses. There are, however, some disadvantages to take into account, such as losing out on potentially larger profits from riskier investments. Rising inflationary situations may also lead savings to lose buying power.

While saving is an important component of any financial plan, a balanced approach to financial planning requires combining saving with other types of investment, such as stock market investing or retirement savings.

Benefits and Drawbacks of Saving:
Pros:
- Creates an emergency reserve
- Finances immediate objectives like purchasing food, a new phone, or a trip.
- Little chance of suffering a loss. Bank savings are covered by FDIC insurance.

Cons
- Significantly reduced yields
- Could suffer from inflation
- Missed opportunities arise from not investing in riskier but more lucrative assets.

What Does Investing Entail?

By putting your money to work in financial instruments like stocks, bonds, and mutual funds, investing allows you to see your money increase over time. Investing, as opposed to saving, entails some risk but also offers the possibility of longer-term, larger returns.

Investing may help you attain long-term financial objectives like retirement, a down payment on a home, or education savings. Selecting assets that fit your objectives, risk tolerance, and time horizon is crucial because investing entails taking on some risk. Since you will have more time to weather the ups and downs of the stock market, you can generally take on more risk the longer you invest.

Let's take an example where you would want to invest in Apple. Purchasing stock in the firm entitles you to a small ownership stake in the development and profitability of the business. The stock in Apple may appreciate over time if the company does well, enabling you to sell it for a profit.

It's crucial to keep in mind that investing has no promises and that there's always a chance of losing money. For instance, your investment may be all but useless if Apple were to file for bankruptcy. To lower your risk, it is crucial to diversify your portfolio by making investments in a range of businesses and sectors.

Chapter 2

Goal-Setting with Money

A crucial first step in achieving financial security is setting short,mid and long-term financial objectives. You'll probably spend more money than you should if you have no clear goals in mind. Then, when you want to retire or when you need money for unforeseen expenses, you won't have enough. You may find yourself in a never-ending cycle of credit card debt and worry that you'll never have enough money for adequate insurance, making you more susceptible than necessary to deal with some of the biggest hazards in life.

As the globe discovered during the epidemic and as many families discover each month, even the most cautious individual cannot be ready for every eventuality. Anticipating future events allows you to analyze potential outcomes and make the best possible preparations for them. This should be a continuous process so that you can adapt your objectives and way of life to the inevitable changes that will occur.

You get the chance to officially examine your objectives, make any necessary updates, and assess your progress from the previous year during your annual financial planning. Take this chance to create objectives if you haven't done so previously to put yourself or yourself and your family on solid financial ground. Financial experts suggest establishing the following objectives, which range from short-term to long-term, to help you learn how to live comfortably within your means, lessen financial difficulties, and save for retirement.

Short-Term Budgetary Objectives

Creating short-term financial goals brings you with the groundwork and confidence boost needed to accomplish longer-term, more ambitious goals. In as short as a year, it should be rather straightforward to complete these initial steps: Make a budget and follow it. Create an emergency savings account. Reduce the amount of debt you owe on your credit card.

- Make a Budget

"Unless you truly know where you are at the moment, you cannot know your destination. That entails creating a budget, according to Lauren Zangardi Haynes, a fee-only and fiduciary financial advisor of Richmond, Virginia's Spark Financial Advisors. "The amount of money that falls through the cracks every month might surprise you."

Using a free budgeting tool like Mint is a simple way to keep track of your expenditures. It will compile all of your account data into one location, allowing you to categorize each spend.

An alternative approach to creating a budget is to comb through your bank records and previous months' invoices, classifying each cost using a spreadsheet or by handwriting it down.

You can make better judgments about where you want your money to go in the future when you can see how you are spending it and use that knowledge as guidance. Do you think dining out is worth the additional cash you spend each month, given its convenience and enjoyment? If so, excellent—that is if you can afford it. If not, you've just learned a simple method for making monthly savings. You may search for methods to save costs while dining out, substitute homemade meals for certain takeaway or restaurant meals, or do both at once.

- Establish an Emergency Fund

You should put aside money in an emergency reserve, especially for unforeseen costs. $500 to $1,000 is a decent starting aim. Once you reach that amount, you should increase it to a point where your emergency fund can handle more severe financial setbacks, including becoming unemployed. You probably wished you had an emergency fund if you didn't have one before the COVID-19 outbreak. Furthermore, you may need to refill it if you have one and have already used it.

- Clear Your Credit Card Debt

On whether to start building an emergency fund or paying off credit card debt first, experts can't agree. Some people advise starting an emergency fund even if you don't already have any credit card debt since any unforeseen costs will push you farther into debt if you don't have one. Some advice paying off credit card debt first since the interest is so expensive and makes reaching other financial objectives much more challenging. Select the philosophy that best resonates with you, or combine elements of both at once.

To pay off credit card debt, Davis suggests making a list of all your obligations ranked from lowest to highest interest rate, then making minimum payments on everything except the highest-rate loan. Make extra payments on your card with the highest interest rate using whatever extra money you have.

The debt avalanche is the name of the strategy Davis outlines. The debt snowball strategy is an additional one to think about. Regardless of the interest rate, you pay off your obligations using the snowball approach from smallest to greatest. The theory behind this is that when you pay off your smallest obligation, you'll feel a feeling of success that will motivate you to pay off your next-smallest bill, and so on, until you're debt-free.

Mid-Term Budgetary Objectives
It is now time to start working toward your mid term financial goals once you have built an emergency fund, paid off your credit card debt, or at least made significant progress toward those three short-term objectives. These

objectives will build a link between your immediate and long-term financial objectives.

- Get Life Insurance and Disability Income Insurance

Do you support your spouse or kids with your income? If so, you should get life insurance to cover them if you die too soon. Term life insurance is the most affordable and least complex kind of life insurance, and it can cover the requirements of most individuals.

You may get the greatest deal on coverage with the assistance of an insurance broker. Most term life insurance companies undertake medical underwriting, and you can undoubtedly find at least one company that will sell you coverage unless you are sick.

- Pay Off Student Loans

Numerous people's monthly budgets are severely impacted by student debt. Reducing or eliminating such payments will free up funds, which can facilitate your retirement savings and other objectives. Refinancing into a new loan with a reduced interest rate is one tactic that might assist you in paying off your student loans. However, exercise caution: Refinancing your federal student loans via a private lender may result in the loss of some of its advantages, including income-based repayment, deferral, and forbearance, all of which may come in handy in difficult circumstances.

- Think About Your Dreams

Midterm objectives might also involve purchasing a first house or, eventually, a vacation property. Perhaps you currently own a house and want to start saving for a bigger one, or perhaps you want to enhance it with some substantial renovations. Other midterm objectives include saving for education or the fees associated with establishing a family.

After deciding on one or more of these objectives, begin calculating the amount of money you'll need to save to get close to achieving them. The first step to realizing your desired future is to visualize it.

Long-Term Budgetary Objectives

Large-scale objectives are often long-term in nature. Achieving these objectives might take years or perhaps decades. Compared to short-term ambitions, your distant goals usually need more funding and consistent attention.

- Retirement fund is an example of a long-term aim.
- Settling a mortgage.
- Launching a company.
- Saving for a child's college fees.

For most individuals, accumulating enough money for retirement is their top long-term financial objective. Generally speaking, you want to set aside between 10% and 15% of each paycheck in a standard IRA Roth IRA, or a tax-advantaged retirement plan such as a 401(k) or 403(b), if you have access to one. However, you must determine the precise amount you'll need to save for retirement to ensure that you are indeed saving enough.

Matching personal objectives with investing strategies

Anyone hoping to ensure a wealthy future must find the correct investing ideas. Developing a successful financial plan requires a thorough comprehension of the many investing strategies as well as the fundamentals of wise investment management.

An Overview of Financial Techniques

A general grasp of the various investing techniques is essential before delving into particular investment strategies. A cautious strategy is chosen by certain investors, who concentrate on low-risk investments like bonds and fixed-income instruments. Some people adopt a more assertive stance, seizing the opportunity to earn more profits from stocks and other assets. You may choose the strategy that most closely matches your risk tolerance and financial objectives by investigating these several approaches.

Investment techniques are essential for helping people reach their financial goals and increase their wealth. They provide a road map for choosing wisely where to put money and how to control risk. Knowing the different investment philosophies will enable you to make well-considered strategic decisions that fit your particular situation.

Value investing is one well-liked investing tactic. This strategy entails looking for cheap stocks or other assets with long-term growth potential. Value investors look closely at market patterns, financial statements, and other pertinent data to find possibilities that the market may have missed. Value investors hope to make large profits over time by buying these assets at a bargain.

However, other investors are more interested in a growth-oriented strategy. Investing in businesses with significant growth potential is the focus of this approach. These businesses could provide cutting-edge goods or services or be involved in developing sectors. Growth investors are prepared to assume greater risk in exchange for the potential for large capital gains. They keep a careful eye on advancements in the industry and market trends to identify businesses that have the potential to grow quickly.

Income-focused methods are an additional investment strategy. These tactics place a high priority on producing steady cash flow via interest and dividend payments. Assets including dividend-paying stocks, bonds, and real estate investment trusts (REITs) are popular choices for income investors. By concentrating on assets that offer regular income, these investors strive to build a consistent stream of cash flow to satisfy their financial demands.

Various Methods for Investing

When it comes to investing, there isn't a single strategy that works for everyone. Every strategy has benefits and downsides of its own. A value investing approach is preferred by certain investors who look for cheap companies with long-term growth potential. Some choose a growth-oriented strategy, emphasizing businesses with significant room for expansion. There are also income-focused strategies that place a higher priority on delivering steady cash flow in the form of interest and dividend payments. Through comprehension of these diverse methodologies, you may customize your investing technique to your objectives and inclinations.

It is noteworthy that investing methods may also be classified according to the degree of risk they include. Certain investors have a cautious approach preference and are risk averse. They place a high priority on capital preservation and are prepared to accept lesser profits in exchange for reduced risk. These investors could devote a significant chunk of their portfolio to fixed-income instruments like AAA corporate bonds or government bonds.

However, some investors feel more at ease accepting greater degrees of risk in the hopes of obtaining perhaps better returns. They could take a more aggressive tack and invest in equities, real estate, or alternative funds like private equity or venture capital. While there is a greater chance of profit with these investments, there is also a greater degree of risk and volatility.

Additionally, investors have the option of using active or passive investing techniques. To outperform the market, active methods include actively managing a portfolio via frequent asset purchases and sales. This strategy requires in-depth investigation, evaluation, and investment oversight. Conversely, passive strategies seek to mimic the performance of a particular asset class or market index. Exchange-traded funds (ETFs) or index funds that follow the performance of a certain market sector are often chosen by passive investors.

Chapter 3

Investment Types

There are undoubtedly many possibilities to invest; for example, changing the tires on your car might be considered an upgrade that will increase the asset's utility and future worth. The popular investment categories listed below are used by individuals to increase their money.

1. Equities/Stocks
   A portion of ownership in a public or private corporation is represented by a share of stock. An investor may be eligible to receive dividend payments from the company's net profit if they hold shares. Its value may also increase and it may be possible to sell it for a profit when the business expands and more investors want to purchase its shares.
   Preferred stock and ordinary stock are the two main categories of equities in which to invest. Voting rights and the ability to participate in certain things are often associated with common stock. Dividends on preferred shares must be paid out

before those on ordinary stock and often have first claim.

Furthermore, equities are often categorized as value or growth investments. Purchasing growth stocks involves investing in a business when it is still in its infancy and before it sees significant success in the market. Purchasing value stocks involves investing in a more established firm whose stock price may not reflect the true worth of the business.

2. Fixed-income securities and bonds
   A bond is an investment that typically requires a one-time payment upfront and periodic payments over the bond's duration. Following that, the investor gets their money back from the bond's maturity. Bond investments are a way for some businesses to raise money, much like debt. Many businesses and government agencies issue bonds, which

investors may purchase to receive a return.

A coupon payment is the periodic sum that bond holders receive. A bond investment's yield is often affected by price fluctuations since the coupon payment is typically set. For instance, if there are market chances to earn 6%, it will become less expensive to purchase a 5% bond; hence, the bond will naturally give a greater yield due to its price decline.

3. Mutual funds and index funds
   Index funds, mutual funds, and other funds combine several assets into a single investment vehicle, eliminating the need to choose individual companies to participate in. Rather than having to independently investigate and choose each firm, an investor may purchase shares of a single mutual fund that has ownership of small-size, developing market companies.

While index funds are often administered passively, mutual funds are actively managed by a company. This indicates that, unlike index funds, which often strive to just replicate or mimic a benchmark, the investing experts managing the mutual fund are attempting to outperform a particular benchmark. Because of this, investing in mutual funds may be more expensive than in more passively structured funds.

4. Real Estate
   Investing in real estate often refers to purchasing actual, physical areas that may be used. It is possible to construct structures on land, occupy office buildings, store merchandise in warehouses, and house families in residential properties. Investing in real estate might include buying ready-to-occupy operational locations or creating sites for particular purposes.

In certain situations, the term "real estate" may refer generally to certain kinds of investments that might produce commodities. An investor may, for instance, purchase farmland, which yields a return dependent on operational revenue and crop output in addition to the increase in the land's value.

5. Commodities
   Raw resources like metals, energy, and agriculture are examples of commodities. Investing in physical commodities such as gold bars is one option available to investors; alternatively, they may choose investment instruments that symbolize digital ownership such as gold exchange-traded funds (ETFs).

   Since commodities are often employed as inputs by society, they might be considered investments. Think about gas, oil, or other energy sources. Businesses sometimes need more energy during times of economic expansion to move more goods or produce more things. Additionally, because of travel, customers can need more energy than usual. In this case, an investor may benefit from fluctuations in the price of commodities.

6. Cryptocurrency
   A blockchain-based money used for holding and transacting digital value is called cryptocurrency. Companies that deal in cryptocurrencies may release tokens or coins that increase in value. These tokens may be used for network transactions or used to pay fees for network transactions.

   On a blockchain, bitcoin may be staked in addition to gaining money. This implies that investors will get more tokens in exchange for agreeing to lock their tokens on a network to aid with transaction validation. Furthermore, decentralized finance—a digital subset of finance that allows individuals to lend money or use it in other ways—has emerged as a result of cryptocurrencies.

7. Collectibles

Acquiring uncommon objects in anticipation of their increasing demand is a less common approach to investing, collecting, or buying collectibles. These tangible things, which range from comic books to sports memorabilia, often need intensive physical maintenance, particularly because older pieces are typically more valuable.

The idea behind collectibles is the same as those of other investment vehicles, including stocks. Both indicate that something will become more well-known in the future. For instance, a contemporary artist could not be well-known, but market interest and worldwide trends and tastes might alter. But if more people become interested in their work over time, their art may be appreciated.

Assembling a diversified portfolio

Purchasing a variety of assets to lower the risk of market volatility is known as diversification, and it is a typical investing strategy. It's a component of asset allocation, which refers to the percentage of a portfolio allocated to different asset types.

The three most popular asset types are cash (or cash equivalents), bonds, and stocks. Investors mix disparate assets (such as stocks and bonds) to attain diversification, preventing an excessive amount of exposure to any one asset class or market segment in their portfolio.

There are several investing alternatives available to investors, and each has pros and cons of its own. Portfolio diversification by asset class, asset class within asset class, and asset class beyond asset class are some of the most popular methods.

An illustration of diversification

Say you put all of your money exclusively in Apple shares (AAPL). Since Apple is a technology business, your asset allocation would consist entirely of equity, or stock, in the market's technology sector. This is a risky strategy because your entire investment portfolio would be negatively impacted if Apple stock prices dropped as a result of unanticipated events. Even if you invest in several tech firms to diversify within the technology sector, your portfolio would still suffer greatly if the whole tech industry were to suffer a downturn.

A portfolio has to be suitably diversified, which means it needs to include equities from a wide range of industries. Even so, to guard against a decline in the stock market as a whole, you may also wish to incorporate bonds or other fixed-income products.

The easiest approach to increase investment returns while lowering risk is via diversification. By deciding against putting all of your money in one place, you shield your portfolio from fluctuations in the market.

Every investor may see diversification in a somewhat different way. To build each portfolio to best suit the unique requirements of each investor, factors including time horizon and risk tolerance should be evaluated case-by-case. Fortunately, there are several resources available to assist in simplifying the process of diversifying your investment accounts.

The advantages of diversification
Diversification raises the possibility of total return while lowering overall risk. This is because some assets will perform well while others will not. However, things could turn over the next year, with the previous underachievers emerging as the new leaders.

Short-term fluctuations in that return are common. Nonetheless, a stock portfolio that is well-diversified usually yields the average historical long-term return of the market. Having a diverse range of assets reduces the likelihood that anyone may negatively impact your portfolio. The disadvantage is that the unexpected profits of a shooting star are never completely realized. The overall consequence of diversity is moderate and steady performance and smoother returns, never jumping up or down too rapidly. The decreased volatility calms down a lot of investors.

The following five pointers will assist you in diversifying:

1. Spread the Wealth: While stocks may be great investments, you shouldn't place all of your money in a single company or industry. Investing in a few firms you know, trust, and

even use daily may help you create your virtual mutual fund.

However, stocks are not the only factor to take into account. Exchange-traded funds (ETFs), real estate investment trusts (REITs), and commodities are other investing options. Additionally, don't limit yourself to your home base. Think globally and beyond it. By spreading your risk this way, you may potentially reap larger benefits.

Some may argue that investing in companies you are familiar with will make regular investors too focused on retail, but getting to know a firm or making use of its products and services may be a positive and healthy way to become involved in this industry.

However, avoid making the mistake of going too far. Make sure you don't exceed a manageable portfolio. Buying a hundred different cars is pointless if you lack the time or money to keep up with the trends. Try to stick to no more than 20 to 30 distinct assets.

2. Examine bond funds or index funds.
You may choose to add fixed-income or index
funds to your portfolio. Purchasing assets that
follow different indices is a great way to
diversify your portfolio over the long run. You
are further protecting your portfolio against
market volatility and unpredictability by
including certain fixed-income options. Rather
than investing in a particular industry, these
funds aim to replicate the performance of broad
indexes by reflecting the value of the bond
market.

Another benefit of these funds is that they often
have cheap costs. It translates to extra cash in
your wallet. Because of the expenses involved in
managing these funds, there are very few
operational and management expenditures.
The fact that index funds are passively managed
may be a disadvantage. Even while passive
investing is often less costly, it may not be the
best option in inefficient markets. For instance,
active management may be advantageous in

fixed-income markets, particularly during difficult economic times.

3. Continue to Expand Your Portfolio
Regularly increase your investment amounts. Utilize dollar-cost averaging if you have $6,000 to invest. The peaks and troughs brought about by market volatility are lessened with the usage of this strategy. By investing the same amount of money over time, the theory behind this technique is to reduce your investment risk.

By using dollar-cost averaging, you may make recurring investments into a predetermined portfolio of stocks. By using this tactic, you will purchase more shares at lower prices and fewer at higher ones.

4. Recognize When to Leave
Both dollar-cost averaging and buying and keeping are wise investments. However, this does not imply you should disregard the dynamics at play just because your assets are managed automatically.

Keep up with your investments and be aware of any changes in the general state of the market. You need to be aware of the progress of the businesses you invest in. You'll be able to determine when to sell, reduce your losses, and move on to your next investment by doing this as well.

5. Pay Close Attention to Commissions
If trading is not your thing, be aware of what you are receiving for your money. While some businesses charge transaction fees, others impose a monthly cost. These have the potential to significantly reduce your revenue.

Know what you are receiving for your money and what you are paying for. Recall that the most economical option isn't usually the best one. Make sure you stay informed about any changes to your costs.

Chapter 4

Examining investing platforms, retirement accounts, and brokerage accounts

An investing account where you may purchase and sell assets is called a brokerage account. You may create a brokerage account on a variety of platforms, and the investments available to you will vary depending on whatever platform you choose. The most widely used brokerage accounts let you trade pooled assets like mutual funds and exchange-traded funds (ETFs) in addition to individual stocks and bonds.

What is the operation of a brokerage account? Consider a brokerage account like any other bank account, with the exception that it may also be used to keep stocks. You may link the account to your bank account and deposit money into it at the time of account opening. The money in your brokerage account may then be used to buy stocks, bonds, mutual funds, and other assets.

Investing carries risk, and financial gain is not a given. However, according to the S&P 500 index, stock market returns have been around 10% yearly on average over the last 150 years. Ideally, your brokerage account's assets will increase over time for you to see.

There are taxes that you could have to pay based on how you make money. For instance, taxes are due when you get profits or interest from your existing assets. When you sell your assets, capital gains taxes can also be due.

The brokerage business executes buy-and-sell orders placed inside your brokerage account on your behalf. The company may charge a fee for this service, which may be expressed as a fixed cost for each transaction or as a percentage of your assets.

There is no limit on the number of taxable brokerage accounts you may create or on the total amount you can invest annually, unlike other forms of investment accounts.

Because they provide a platform for the purchase and sale of a variety of financial products, brokerage accounts are crucial tools for investors.

Brokerage Account Types:

- Single investors may open individual brokerage accounts through which they can trade stocks, bonds, mutual funds, and other assets.

- Joint brokerage accounts allow for joint ownership and collaborative investing choices. They are usually opened by couples.
- Online Brokerages: For self-directed investors, these platforms provide an intuitive user interface. They often provide access to research tools and have reduced rates.
- Conventional Brokerages: They could provide more comprehensive financial services as well as tailored guidance. Their fees could be more, however.

Retirement accounts are specific investment vehicles created to provide tax benefits while assisting people in saving for their future.

Individuals with earned income may utilize an individual retirement account (IRA) to save for retirement while taking advantage of certain tax benefits. The IRA is largely intended for independent contractors who lack access to corporate retirement plans, such as the 401(k), which are solely offered by employers.

Typical retirement funds consist of:

- 401(k):

Retirement account provided by the employer.
Pre-tax money is commonly used for contributions.
Certain companies match donations made by their employees.
growth that is delayed and withdrawals that are taxed when you retire.
- Account for Individual Retirement (IRA):

Tax benefits for individual retirement accounts.

Contributions to traditional IRAs are tax deductible, and their growth is tax deferred. Contributions to Roth IRAs are made after taxes, but retirement withdrawals are tax-free.

- Plans for Self-Employed Retirement:

Options for independent contractors or small company owners include the Solo 401(k) and Simplified Employee Pension (SEP) IRA. provide tax benefits like those found in conventional retirement plans.

Benefits to taxes:

- Tax Deductions: You may be able to deduct contributions to conventional retirement funds from your taxes.
- Tax-Free Growth: Tax-deferred or tax-free growth on assets is a feature of many retirement plans.
- Penalty-Free Withdrawals: Certain retirement plans provide withdrawals without incurring penalties for certain

uses, such as a first-time house purchase or approved educational costs.

Other Websites for Investing:

- Robotic Advisors:

platforms for automated investing that build and maintain diverse portfolios using algorithms. usually charge less than more conventional financial counselors.

- Platforms for Peer-to-Peer Lending:

Permit people to give each other direct loans of money.
provide a chance to earn more returns than standard savings accounts.

- Property Crowdfunding:

platforms that let people put smaller amounts of money into real estate ventures.

offers real estate diversity without requiring the acquisition of full properties.

- Exchanges for cryptocurrencies:

platforms for trading, purchasing, and selling cryptocurrencies such as Ethereum and Bitcoin. Due to its high volatility and speculative nature, caution is advised.

- Plans for Employee Stock Purchases (ESPP):

offered by some businesses to enable staff members to buy company shares at a reduced cost.
maybe a kind of long-term investment connected to a job.

Chapter 5

Stock Market Fundamentals

The Stock Market: What Is It?

Stock market shows several marketplaces where shares of publicly traded corporations are bought and sold. Official exchanges and over-the-counter (OTC) markets who adhere to strict guidelines are used for these financial transactions.

Stock exchanges make up the larger stock market, traders in the stock market buy or sell shares.

The New York Stock Exchange (NYSE) and the Nasdaq are the two main stock exchanges in the United States.

Comprehending the Stock Market
Securities buyers and sellers may meet, communicate, and deal on the stock market. The markets function as a measurement for the economy as a whole and enables discovery of price for company shares. A fair price, great liquidity, and transparency are guaranteed to buyers and sellers as players in the free market compete.

The Workings of the Stock Market
Market participants may trade shares and other qualifying financial products in a safe, regulated environment with little to no operational risk on the stock market. The major and secondary stock markets function under the regulations set out by the regulatory body.

By way of an initial public offering (IPO), the stock market, as a primary market, enables corporations to issue and sell their shares to the public for the first time. This process assists businesses in getting the funding they need from investors.

A business splits up into several shares, which it then sells to the general public at a set price per share.

To enable this process, a corporation requires a marketplace where these shares may be sold and this is provided via the stock market. A listed business may later on, through rights issues or follow-on offerings, among other methods, provide fresh, extra shares through other offerings. They may even repurchase or remove their shares.

Owners of firm shares will do so with the hope that either the value of their shares will increase or that they will get dividend payments, or both. The firm and its partners pay the stock market a fee for their services as an architect of this capital-raising process.

Investors may also trade assets they already possess on stock exchanges in a market known as the secondary market.

What Roles Do Stock Markets Play?

Price findings,, liquidity, price lucidity and fair dealings in trading endeavors are all warranted by the stock market.

The stock market helps ensure that assets are priced fairly and transparently by providing data for every buy and sell order to interested parties. Substantially, the market endeavors that the right purchase and sell orders are matched correctly.

Price discovery, in which all stock buyers and sellers work together to establish a stock's price, is a function that stock markets must provide. Orders should be placed instantly by those who are competent and eager to trade, and the market will make sure that the orders are filled at a reasonable price.

Investors, traders, explorers,and hedgers are examples of stock market traders. A trader may enter and leave a position in a matter of seconds, but an investor may purchase equities and keep them for a long time. Although a hedger may engage in derivatives trading, a market maker supplies the essential liquidity in the market.

Who Assists in Stock Market Trading for Investors?

Stock brokers buy and sell stocks on behalf of investors, they serve as middlemen between stock exchanges and investors. Portfolio managers are specialists in investing client portfolios, which are a group of safe futures. Investment bankers act as a company's representative in a variety of contexts, including ongoing mergers and acquisitions or private businesses looking to go public via an initial public offering (IPO).

Techniques for purchasing and disposing of stocks

One of the most common strategies to invest your money and increase your wealth is to buy and sell stocks. However, how can one determine when to purchase and when to sell? Which are the best approaches to reduce risks and increase returns? We'll look at some of the most popular and successful stock trading strategies in this post, along with some advice to help you make more informed choices.

1. Know your objectives.
Before beginning your stock trading, you should be quite clear about your objectives. Do you want to focus on short-term earnings, long-term growth, or both? To what extent are you prepared to take a risk? To what extent are you prepared to commit time and energy to doing research and analysis? You may choose the best course of action for your circumstances by considering the answers to these questions. For instance, you could choose to invest in dividend-paying, stable, and diversified firms if you're

hoping for long-term growth. You may wish to trade more regularly and take advantage of market volatility if you are seeking short-term rewards.

2. Observe the patterns

Following trends is one of the simplest and most popular methods for buying and selling stocks. This implies that you should sell declining equities and purchase rising ones. The concept is to ride the market's movement rather than keeping equities that are depreciating. You must employ technical analysis, which is the study of price movements, patterns, and indicators, to track the trends. You can determine levels of support and resistance as well as entry and departure points with the use of technical analysis. But you also need to be mindful of the dangers associated with following trends, such as volatility, reversals, and misleading signals.

3. Purchase cheap, sell high

Buying cheap and selling high is another popular and easy stock trading method. This implies that you sell expensive equities and purchase discounted ones. The concept is to take advantage of the market's inefficiencies and make money on the discrepancy between the stocks' perceived and true values. Fundamental analysis, which examines a company's financial performance, competitive advantage, and growth potential, is necessary if you want to purchase cheap and sell high. You may ascertain the stocks' intrinsic worth and prospects with the use of fundamental research. The drawbacks of purchasing cheap and selling high, such as timing, opportunity cost, and market mood, must also be considered.

4. Increase portfolio diversification. Diversifying your portfolio is one of the most crucial and successful stock-buying and selling tactics. This implies that you distribute your investment over a variety of marketplaces, industries, sectors, and stock kinds. The

objective is to improve your chances of generating steady returns while lowering your exposure to any one risk element. You must take into account several criteria, including your time horizon, financial goals, and risk tolerance, to diversify your portfolio. Additionally, you must regularly review and rebalance your portfolio and make adjustments in response to changing circumstances.

5. Study with the professionals

Learning from the pros is one of the most beneficial and profitable stock-buying and selling tactics. This implies that you heed the counsel, observations, and suggestions of seasoned and prosperous traders, analysts, and investors. The objective is to both avoid their errors and gain from their experience, expertise, and talents. You should study books, articles, blogs, podcasts, and newsletters on stock trading, investing, and economics if you want to learn from the pros. It is also necessary to employ critical thinking and independent judgment, as well as to evaluate and contrast various points of view.

6. Control your emotions

Controlling your emotions is one of the most difficult but important stock trading tactics. This implies that you don't allow regret, fear, greed, or hope to sway your choices. The notion is that you make decisions based on logic, facts, and evidence impartially and logically. You must have a trading plan, which is a set of regulations outlining your objectives, criteria, and approach, to control your emotions. A trading diary, which is a log of your transactions, outcomes, and thoughts, is also essential. You may maintain accountability, discipline, and concentration by keeping a trading notebook and a trading strategy.

Chapter 6

Investment in Bonds

Bonds, also referred to as fixed-income instruments, are used by businesses or governments to borrow money from investors. Typically, bonds are issued to generate money for certain initiatives. The bond issuer agrees to repay the investment over a certain period, plus interest.

When you purchase bonds, you are effectively lending money to the bond issuer, who has promised to return your money and pay you interest at a later period. Although bonds are seldom covered by the media more than stocks are, the global bond market has a higher market capitalization than the equities market. Global bond markets were expected to be worth $102.8 trillion in 2018, while global stock markets were assessed to be worth $74.7 trillion by the Securities Industry and Financial Markets Association (SIFMA) in 2018.

Bonds: What Are They?

Bonds are financial instruments in which a purchaser loans money to a business or the government for a period of time in return for annual interest payments. The bond issuer compensates the investor's funds at the bond's full growth. Bonds are sometimes referred to as fixed income since your investment will provide set payments throughout the bond.

Businesses issue bonds to fund new businesses, acquisitions. Bond sales are a means for governments to raise additional funds in addition to their tax collection. Upon buying a bond, you are now a debtor for the company giving the bond.

Bonds are an essential part of a well-diversified investment portfolio as many of them, particularly investment-grade bonds, are lower-risk investments than stocks. Bonds may preserve wealth while offering a consistent income stream throughout your retirement years and act as a risk hedge against more volatile assets like equities.

Credit rating organizations provide ratings to certain bond categories, such as government and corporate bonds, to assess the bonds' quality. The probability that investors will get their money back is determined in part by these ratings. Bond ratings are usually classified into two main categories: lower-rated high-yield bonds and higher-rated investment-grade bonds.

Corporate, municipal, and Treasury bonds are the three main categories of bonds:

A firm may issue corporate bonds as a means of
raising money for projects like growth, R&D, or
expansion. You must pay taxes on interest
received from business bonds. To make up for
this drawback, corporate bonds often have
greater yields than municipal or government
bonds.

A city, municipality, or state may issue
municipal bonds to generate funds for
infrastructure projects including roads, hospitals,
and schools. The interest you receive from
municipal bonds is tax-free, in contrast to
corporate bonds. Municipal bonds come in two
types: revenue and general obligation.

- General obligation bonds are used by
  municipalities to finance non-income-
  generating projects like parks and
  playgrounds. The issuer of general
  obligation bonds is permitted to take all
  necessary steps, including increasing
  taxes, to ensure bond payments since the

bonds are guaranteed by the full faith and credit of the issuing municipality.

- Revenue bonds, on the other hand, pay back investors with the revenue they're anticipated to earn. For instance, if a state sells revenue bonds to pay for a new roadway, it would pay investors using the money collected from tolls. Federal taxes do not apply to either general obligation or revenue bonds, and state and local taxes sometimes do not apply to local municipal bonds as well. Revenue bonds are an excellent method to raise money and support a community.

The United States government issues Treasury bonds, or T-bonds as they are commonly called. Treasury bonds are regarded as risk-free since the US government backs them with its whole faith and credit. However, the interest rates on government bonds are lower than those on corporate bonds. Treasury bonds are free from state and municipal taxes, but they are subject to federal taxation.

What are some tips for bond investing?

When making bond investments, it's critical to:

1. Understand when bonds mature. The day on which you will get your money back is known as the maturity date. Find out how long your investment will be locked in the bond before you commit any money.
2. Ascertain the bond's rating. The rating of a bond shows its creditworthiness. The likelihood that the bond will fail and you will lose your investment increases with a lower grade. According to Standard & Poor's rating system, the highest rating is AAA. The largest default risk is associated with low-quality or junk bonds, which are defined as any bond with a rating of C or worse.
3. Examine the history of the bond issuer. When choosing whether or not to invest in

a company's bonds, it might be useful to know about its history.

4. Recognize the risks you can tolerate. Because they carry more risk, bonds with a lower credit rating usually have higher yields. Consider your risk tolerance carefully, and don't make investments based just on yield.

5. Consider macroeconomic hazards. Bonds lose value as interest rates increase. The possibility that interest rates may shift before the bond matures is known as interest rate risk. But don't attempt to time the market; it's hard to forecast changes in interest rates. Rather, concentrate on your long-term financial goals. A further danger to bonds is rising inflation.

6. Bolster your overarching financial goals. Bonds are a good way to balance out your stock and other asset-class investments and diversify your portfolio. Use an asset allocation calculator related to age to ensure that your portfolio is well balanced.

7. Carefully read the prospectus. Make sure you research the costs and the specific sorts of bonds included in the fund if you're investing in a bond fund. Only a portion of the narrative may be revealed by the fund's name; for instance, government bond funds can include non-government bonds.

8. Employ a bond specialist broker. If you are buying individual bonds, choose a bond market-savvy company. To identify reliable experts who can assist you in opening a brokerage account, use FINRA BrokerCheck.

9. Find out about any commissions and costs. Your broker can assist you in deciphering the costs related to your investment.

What are the advantages of bond investing?

Bonds have many benefits, including:

- Capital preservation refers to safeguarding your investment's total worth via assets that provide a primary return. Because bonds normally carry less risk than stocks, these assets might be a viable alternative for investors with less time to recover losses.
- Revenue generation: The coupon payments received from bonds give a set amount of revenue regularly.
- Diversification: You may create a portfolio that seeks returns but is robust in all market conditions by investing in a mix of stocks, bonds, and other asset types. Bonds tend to be more attractive during periods of stock market decline because of the general negative connection between stocks and bonds.
- Risk management: It's generally accepted that fixed-income investments are less

risky than equities. This is thus because macroeconomic risks like economic downturns and geopolitical catastrophes often have less of an impact on fixed-income assets.

- Invest in your city: You may support your community by purchasing municipal bonds. Even while these bonds may not return as much as a corporate bond, they are often used to fund the construction of hospitals, schools, or other facilities that raise people's standards of living.

What dangers come with investing in bonds?

Purchasing bonds have risks, just like any other investment:

- Interest rate risk: Bond prices decrease when interest rates increase, potentially resulting in the loss of value of the bonds you now own. The primary factor causing price volatility in bond markets is changes in interest rates.

- Risk of inflation: The rate of increase in the cost of goods and services over time is known as inflation. An investor's buying power is diminished if inflation surpasses the fixed-income yield of a bond.

- Credit risk: Credit risk, which is the potential for an issuer to miss payments on its debt, is often referred to as business risk or financial risk.

- The chance that an investor may want to sell a bond but not be able to find a buyer is known as liquidity risk.

- Bonds typically provide lower returns than stocks do. Between 1928 and 2010, the average return on equities was 11.3%, while the average return on bonds was 5.28%.

- Bonds set a temporal limit on how long your money may be frozen. For instance, you cannot redeem a 10-year bond that you have purchased for ten years. This gives rise to the possibility of your original investment depreciating. On the other hand, stocks are always tradable. By spreading out your portfolio's assets, you may reduce these risks.

Chapter 7

Exchange-traded funds and Mutual funds

Mutual funds and exchange-traded funds (ETFs) are similar financial instruments. These kinds of funds are a well-liked method for investors to diversify since they are made up of a variety of diverse assets. ETFs and mutual funds vary significantly from one another, despite their numerous similarities. One significant distinction between the two is that mutual funds may only be bought at the close of each trading day at a price determined by a formula called net asset value, but exchange-traded funds (ETFs) can be exchanged intraday like stocks.

The first mutual fund was introduced in 1924, and they have been in existence in their current form for over a century. With the introduction of the first ETF in January 1993, exchange-traded funds are comparatively recent additions to the investing scene.

While ETFs were often passively managed and followed market indexes or particular sector indices, the majority of mutual funds in the past were actively managed, meaning that fund managers made choices on how to allocate assets inside the fund. The line between the two has been less clear in recent years as investors have access to an increasing number of actively managed exchange-traded funds (ETFs) while a significant number of mutual fund assets are held by passive index funds.

Mutual Funds

Mutual funds have larger minimum investment demands than ETFs. These minimums may change based on the fund type and business. For instance, a $3,000 minimum investment is needed for the Vanguard 500 Index Investor Fund Admiral Shares, but a $250 first deposit is needed for American Funds' Growth Fund of America.

A team or fund manager actively manages several mutual funds, choosing which stocks or other assets to purchase and sell to beat the market and maximize returns for investors. These funds are often more expensive since the time, labor, and resources needed for the investigation and analysis of securities are much greater.

Mutual fund purchases and sales happen directly between investors and the fund. When net asset value (NAV) is calculated after the business day, the price of the fund is established.

Different Mutual Fund Types
Mutual funds are categorized legally into two categories: open-ended and closed-end. The fund shares are where the varieties differ from one another.

- Funds with No Close

In terms of volume and managed assets, these funds dominate the mutual fund industry. The purchasing and selling of funds happens between investors and the fund company in open-ended funds. The fund can issue a no limit number of shares. Therefore, more shares are issued when more investors finance the fund.

The daily marking-to-market procedure, mandated by federal rules, is a valuation process that modifies the fund's per-share price to reflect changes in the portfolio (asset) value. The quantity of shares that are outstanding does not affect the value of a person's shares.

- Closed-End Investments

These funds only issue a certain amount of shares; when investor demand increases, they stop issuing additional shares.

Demand from investors pushes prices instead of the fund's net asset value (NAV). Share purchases are often done at or below NAV.

Exchange-Traded Funds (ETFs): For an entry-level investment, ETFs may be purchased for as low as one share plus any applicable fees or charges. Institutional investors establish or redeem ETFs in bulk, and the shares trade amongst investors all day long much as stocks do. ETFs are tradable short, just as stocks are. Long-term investors are not very interested in such provisions, but traders and speculators find them vital. However, since the market sets the price of ETFs continually, trading may occur at a price different from the real NAV, which might provide a chance for arbitrage.

ETFs provide investors with tax benefits. ETFs (and index funds) as passively managed portfolios often earn lower capital gains than actively managed mutual funds.

ETF Structures
ETFs come in three different structures:

- Exchange-Traded Open-End Fund: Under the SEC's Investment Company Act of 1940, the great majority of ETFs are registered as open-end management firms.

There are certain restrictions for diversification with this ETF structure. For instance, shares of a single stock cannot make up more than 5% of the portfolio.

Compared to the Unit Investment Trust structure, this structure provides more flexibility in portfolio management since it does not need to completely duplicate an index. Therefore, several open-end ETFs utilize optimization or sampling algorithms to duplicate an index and match its features, rather than holding every single component securities in the index. Dividends received by open-end funds may also be reinvested in other assets up to shareholder distributions. Lending of securities is permitted, and the fund may use derivatives.

- A unit investment trust that is exchange-traded (UIT). The Investment Company Act of 1940 also applies to exchange-traded UITs; however, to reduce tracking error, they must completely replicate their respective indexes, cap investments in a single issue at 25% or less, and establish extra weighting limitations for diversified and non-diversified funds.

The SPDR S&P 500 ETF, like other early ETFs, had a UIT-style structure. UITs pay cash dividends every quarter instead of automatically reinvested dividends.

They are not permitted to possess derivatives or participate in securities lending.

- Grantor trust traded on an exchange. For commodity-focused exchange-traded funds (ETFs), this is the ideal form. These ETFs are set up as grantor trusts, which are not registered under the Investment Company Act of 1940 but are registered under the Securities Act of 1933. Though the underlying shares of the company the ETF invests in are owned by the investor, this kind of ETF is quite similar to a closed-ended fund. This involves exercising the voting privileges that come with stock holdership. However, the fund's makeup remains unchanged. Dividends are given to shareholders immediately; they are not reinvested. Trading must be done in quantities of 100 shares. Among these ETFs is Holding Company Depository Receipts (HOLDRs).

Chapter 8

Formulating Your Investment Plan

Any successful investment manager has a documented, quantifiable, and repeatable investing strategy in place. But a lot of investors just move about, without really spending any time developing and evaluating their overall plans.

The guidelines that follow will assist you in developing a sustainable investing plan. In theory, this should result in more reliable performance and less emotional investing choices.

Above all, it will assist in preventing a disorganized portfolio of discrete assets that, when considered together, lack a unifying theme or goal. The four phases of developing an investing plan are listed below.

1. Put It in Writing

Documenting your investing plan in writing is the first step in the process. Famous author and management quality expert Dr. W. Edwards Deming once said, "If you can't explain what you are doing as a procedure, you don't know what you are doing."

It is crucial to put your investing plan in writing, just like anything else that calls for a methodical approach. This will assist you in expressing it. You should review your plan once it has been created to ensure that it still aligns with your long-term investing goals. By putting your plan in writing, you'll have something to fall back on during chaotic situations and be less likely to make rash financial choices.

It also provides you with something to analyze and adjust if you find errors or your investing goals change. Having a defined plan can aid customers in understanding your investing process if you are a professional investor. In addition to reducing customer questions and improving client retention, this may boost trust.

2. Hold Convictions

You ought to have opinions about what causes investments to become overpriced or undervalued, as well as strategies for taking advantage of them. This includes your opinion on the efficiency of the investing markets. What distinguishes me from the market as a smarter person? "What distinguishes me as a competitor?"

You could be privy to unique research that not many other investors are, or you might possess unique industry expertise. Or maybe you think that you can take advantage of certain market abnormalities, such as purchasing companies with cheap price-to-book ratios. After determining what your competitive edge is, the next step is to determine how to implement a long-term trading strategy successfully to take advantage of it.

You should have guidelines in your trading strategy for both purchasing and selling assets. Additionally, bear in mind that if other investors adopt the same method, your competitive edge may soon lose its profitability.

Conversely, you may think that because there is no persistent competitive advantage for any investor, the investment markets are entirely efficient. In this scenario, investing passively in index funds is a good way to concentrate your approach on reducing taxes and transaction expenses.

3. Give It Sturdiness

The ability of an investing plan to perform effectively in every kind of market scenario is a critical component. A competent investment manager can articulate the advantages and disadvantages of their approach and can explain where their investment success originates from.

Many excellent investing methods may have periods of strong success followed by periods of lagged performance as market trends and economic cycles shift. Even if your technique is momentarily out of style, it is essential to remain confident and invest with conviction if you have a clear grasp of its shortcomings. It may also assist you in identifying tactics that could support your own. A common illustration of this is combining growth and value investment approaches.

4. Take A Measure

You can't truly comprehend or improve upon something you can't measure. As a result, you need to have a baseline by which to gauge how successful your investing plan is. Your investing approach and your benchmark should complement each other. Your investment aim should also fit your benchmark.

Relative and absolute benchmarks are the two most used kinds of financial benchmarks. A passive market index, such as the S&P 500 Index or the Bloomberg US Aggregate Bond Index, is an example of a relative benchmark. A desired return, like 6% yearly, would be an example of an absolute benchmark.

Chapter 9

Investing in Ethics and Sustainability

The concept of utilizing one's own money to contribute positively to society is referred to as ethical and sustainable investment. Although the phrases are interchangeable, you may also hear it referred to as impact investing or socially responsible investing.

Almost any investment that is undertaken to improve society in any manner may be considered ethical and sustainable, regardless of whether it is done so from the perspective of political activity, environmental effect, social transformation, or religious views. It is crucial to remember that everyone has a different idea of what constitutes an ethical or sustainable practice.

People may earn from ethical and sustainable investments while also having a good influence on the future. Ethical investing only entails being more knowledgeable about the businesses, indices, or even commodities that one is investing in. It does not, by any means, contradict the notion that investments should be profitable for traders or investors.

Ethical investing: what is it?

A key goal of ethical investing is to achieve both positive returns and the investor's moral, religious, and societal ideals. Many investors are beginning to demand that the firms they invest in be socially responsible, as dubious and unlawful investment arrangements become more prevalent. This entails showing respect to their staff, producing wholesome goods and services, and abstaining from immoral business methods.

Who Will Invest Ethically?

Investors who want to utilize their money to support worthy causes may consider ethical investment. An investor might, for instance, steer clear of tobacco firms or hold interests in those that manufacture tobacco if they believe that tobacco is harmful.

Different Ethical Investment Types

1. Investment funds with a social conscience (SRI Funds)

Investments in contentious industries including gambling, guns, cigarettes, alcohol, and oil are avoided by SRI funds. In this case, choosing investments requires careful consideration of the investor's moral values.

2. Funds for the environment, society, and governance (ESG Funds)

ESG funds, as opposed to SRI funds, take into account the potential tangible effects that environmental, social, and governance risks and opportunities may have on a company's performance when making investment decisions. They can make investments in sustainability and still get the same kind of returns as they would from a conventional strategy.

3. Funds for Impact
Fund performance is equally important to impact funds. As a result, they actively seek to promote businesses that provide certain goods and services by enacting ethical improvements. Impact funds are suited for investors who are socially concerned but also desire strong returns.

4. Funds Based on Faith
Faith-based funds rigorously exclude investments that do not fall into this category and only make investments in equities that adhere to religious principles and aspirations.

Benefits of Ethical Investment

When an ethical holding company does well, the investor is pleased. They gain both financially and emotionally when the business aligns with their ideals.

The future growth of investments in ethical funds has the potential to be significant as more individuals make them.

The increasing prominence of ethical investment will incentivize other companies to enhance their ethical standards to get capital.

Drawbacks of Ethical Investing

Since ethical investing is not a passive approach, it requires extensive due diligence to make sure the investor's values and beliefs are aligned with the plan.

Since ethical investing may not provide the best returns, the investor forgoes financial gain in favor of an ethical strategy.

Due to the study required to choose the best investment, ethical investing may come with higher costs.

Is Ethical Investing Successful?

One main purpose of ethical investors is to avoid investing in firms that generate items that are against the social, moral, and religious beliefs of the investor. But just because you choose not to invest in a bad firm doesn't mean that money isn't still flowing to the company.

When a stock is bought by an investor, the money goes to the seller, who is a private investor rather than the business. Only when it issues new shares via an IPO does the firm make a profit. As a result, moral investors do not penalize the bad businesses.

Also, by boycotting a firm, ethical investors are restricting the pool of possible shareholders which may decrease the price of the stocks, this just makes it more tempting to unethical investors in the market to acquire the shares at these reduced rates.

Society benefits from ethical investment, but it must meet specific requirements that are difficult to meet.

Finding a profitable company concept that benefits everyone is necessary. One example of an ethical investment is solar panels. It is counterproductive, however, to support a solar panel manufacturer that contaminates the environment throughout the production process. If the investor can find a business opportunity that will result in a beneficial influence on the world, then there has to be "additionality" - a route by which the business may lead the firm to expand sustainably. In the stock market, achieving this goal is more challenging.

Refusing to invest in immoral enterprises doesn't imply they will go away; in fact, they can thrive since there will always be new investors looking for large profits.

Does Ethical Investing Work

Investing ethically has benefits. It does assist businesses in obtaining funding so they may expand and support their corporate social responsibility (CSR) initiatives. Additionally, it provides investors with the power to align firm operations and procedures with their ethical standards and beliefs.

Although there may be a trade-off in terms of decreased portfolio returns, this is still worth it given the other advantages.

When an investor wants to impact society, they choose ethical investing. Meeting their moral, social, and religious ideals is their main objective when investing; profits are a secondary consideration.

Although ethical investing has many benefits, it is a costly approach since it requires extensive study to identify assets that align with the investor's main objective. Furthermore, investing in unethical companies won't stop them from succeeding because other investors looking for returns will continue to support them.

Conclusion

Investing Made Easy: A Step-by-Step Handbook for Beginners" is an empowering experience that gives inexperienced investors the skills and self-assurance they need to successfully navigate the complicated world of finance. It is imperative that, as we wrap up this guidebook, we consider the important ideas and realizations that emerged from each chapter.

Keep in mind that investing is a lifetime endeavor. Your financial objectives could change, and there will be new possibilities and obstacles in the market. This manual provides a strong foundation of information that enables you to confidently pursue your financial goals, adjust to changes, and make well-informed choices.

The investment world is ever-changing, and your financial path is distinct to you. "Investing Made Easy" is your travel companion, providing advice and insights throughout the thrilling journey to financial freedom and development. The guidelines in this manual are intended to assist you at every stage, whether your objective is to save for a particular occasion, prepare for retirement, or create wealth that will last generations.

It's time to put your learning into practice now that you have the knowledge and self-assurance to do so. Make a careful strategy for your investments, maintain your discipline, and acknowledge your accomplishments as you go. You are responsible for your financial future.